The Lost Ghosts of Lemnos
Renderings and Renditions

ISBN: ISBN: 979-8-218-76810-2
marrowstone press, All rights reserved.

Back cover image: "Dream Inspection," galenograph, Galen Garwood 2025

The Lost Ghosts of Lemnos
Renderings and Renditions

Peter Nissen Weltner

> But now
> Draw in your head, alone and too tall here.
> Your eyes already in the slant of drifting foam;
> Your breath sealed by the ghosts I do not know:
> Draw in your head and sleep the long way home.
>
> Hart Crane, Voyages V

marrowstone press

To:

Atticus Carr
Robert Mohr
Galen Garwood
Clarinda Harriss
David Morris
Susan Crowl
Jon O'Bergh
Lindley Young
Nancy McDermid
Galen Williams
Benda Hillman:

Thank you.

Table of Contents

I.

II.

III.

I

Europe

Zeus came to me as a black bull in a meadow where
he stole me from my withered father, raped me
in a field of poppies, chrysanthemum, pink
clover. Look at me. Do you believe I'd dare
tempt a god? He promised me immortality,
but look at me, look at me. Can you still think
I bore him three sons, wrinkled as I am, and ugly?
But I did. Minos, Crete's tyrant, killer of so many
children he was made king over the dead. Then
immortal Rhadamanthys who in his reckless cruelty
cruelly punishes the ill-fated forever. And Sarpedon,
born for war, driven to destroy, slaughter every one
of the Trojans with his swords, sharp lances, shiny spears
until Ilium fell into the smoldering ruins history still sheds tears
for. It is dreadful thing for a woman to mother a god's children,
to be the bearer of death. The imperium to come the world most fears.

(After the only surviving fragment from Aeschylus' play, Europa)

Prometheus

Ouranos' Titanic offspring, distant giant race, see
one of your blood-kin bound on a mountain's
cliff, fettered by iron chains, like a ship in stormy
waters moored in port against torrential rains
and lightning flashes endangering its voyage,
the sea roaring, crashing boats on rocks,
the sailors in harbor, fearful of divine rage,
god-like powers, refusing to risk what ill-luck's
left them to dare the waves till the storm's
over: thus is Prometheus trapped, caught, stuck.
Cronos's son, Zeus, has condemned him, fettered
him there, fastened him, against all holy norms,
to those granitic icy stones, aided by the art
of Hephaestus riveting his limbs, driving cruel
bolts through his body. Zeus' torture has come to rule,

power against power, and you reduced to impotence.
Prometheus is transfixed, transfigured by pain, by
a Titan's monumental suffering. Here, all is silence
except for the buzz and hum and insect cry
and bite of the Furies. Eagle Zeus with his hooked
talons, pursues him, devours his tasty liver,
gnaws it as it swells back to size, fatted
when eaten, mutilation now an insidious reviver
of his agony, his unending pain. Who would not
long for death? But the woeful foe, transgressor
cannot die, must endure, bear witness to the ancient
dolorous anguish of the first gift-giving revolutionary:
this fire-bringer, this creator. See, rendered by the centuries,
how he remains fastened upon the body of humanity, only
his tears, like ice melting off the Caucasus, freed from enchainment.

(After a fragment from a lost Prometheus by Aeschylus transcribed into
Latin by Cicero)

2

Oedipus Arrives in Thebes

It's like living ancient snapshots. Casting linen on his body.
Crossing the sea's plains, listening to the dolphins'
song. Hurling the shaft with its point forked. Journeying
to Crete to hear its bull bellow women's sorrows. Who wins

a fine maiden such as those in Thebes is sure to breed.
Seated on her father's tomb, Niobe mourns for
her children. Burn Amphion's house, destroy his seed,
you fire-bearing eagles of Zeus for that is what gods adore,

shafts of pine trees ablaze with fire, stabs of godly Frenzy,
a scorpion's sting.
            We were coming to the end of our
long journey when the way suddenly divided into three
roads where I killed an old wretched thief. Every hour

since, I breathe a fevered sleep. By reason of what destiny
did I slay him in anger? Why have I suffered piteously
for that old man with a stick, legs cramped by pain, deluded
by my ingenuity? Lamentation is the only way the unsaid

gets said. The mark of men is to be wise and just in any calamity.
Demeter, soul-nourisher, let me be worthy of your mysteries,
red poppies and barley, ears of wheat, olive groves, dark pine trees,
while I re-open Thebes' plagued gates, sent there in this matter of the sacred.

(After scattered fragments from Aeschylus)

The Thebans Say Goodbye to Their King

O how piteous they are, the unkind ages
through which life fatally passes,
birth to death, none of it meaning
anything. Think of the last breath
a man struggles to take. Why?
He's afraid. No one can say
joy is not fleeting, does not fade
like dreams into night's bleak emptiness.

Miserable man, devoted to sorrow,
now you know, at last, why no man
can say he's blessed until his life
is over. Stained, shamed by crimes
too awful to name, you, in your pride,
knew glory, your best days by
solving the riddles of that claw-hooked,
winged, lion-haunched she-beast
of destiny, saving us from plague until you fell.

You'd towered over Thebes' seven gates.
We praised you, made you our king,
our mighty authority. Now we wonder
if there ever was such a man, see
you, in agony, married to nothing
but pain, you, your father having plowed
the same field, furrowed it, harvested
its crops, the unspeakable seeds you'd planted
there born doomed, engendered to the one grief.

Kairos, with its cosmic eyes that see all,
has exposed us to your monstrosity,
chimerical confusions of generations,
the chaos that's fallen upon us,
father-son, son-father. Listen to how
we wail for you, mourn you, living
as if already dead, you who gave
us life and breath, freed our city, then cast it
back to night, blind as you were, blinded as you'll be.

O people of Thebes, our countrymen, look
on him, the genius, we'd all agreed,
of the morning, noon, night of our lives.
We'd envied him, were jealous of his glory.
Yet number no one happy until after
the death that ends all pain. We'd loved you
once. But, like a boat on a stormy black
sea, our city now breaks apart on the rocky
shores of the fate we share with you, dear father.

    (After Sophocles)

Theseus

I am ram and ox, sword and ax,
blood, knife, wood, fire.
I am a riddle to ask
me. "Are you hate or desire?"

I am the lies I told you
about my life's story,
none of it true,
no more than history

is. I am too old to care,
yet want it told,
would dare
to tell it, give gold

to you if you'd listen. I am
the ulcer that feeds
off flesh, not a new-born lamb
whose random deeds

excuse themselves. May a heron
in flight, on high,
drop upon
me its dung out of the sky

to smite me, a serpent uncoil
to bite my foot.
(My blood will boil,
my skin turn to ice.) May a brute

from the wild middle seas swallow
me, aged, desolate, and scant
of hair. What sorrow
is mine, you trouble me with, faint

of heart. I had my beloved son
Hippolytus
killed by Poseidon.
had him drowned in the abyss

of his innocence, his luxurious
locks, like those of girls,
blond and lustrous,
golden with curls,

soft and generous to touch,
like Pirithous'
hair that I would reach
out to fondle, kiss,

until it became as unimaginable,
as unbearable, Phaedra, my son,
in love, and I incapable
of holding on

to either, I, who owned four horses
under yoke, nostrils
bound with fluted muzzles
that my son chose

to drive into the sea
only
to lose
control like me, maddened by

jealousy, who gave him life,
who chose to destroy
it, throat and knife,
boy and father.

    (After a brief fragment from Aeschylus)

7

The Tomb of Aeschylus

1.

The Mysians' boundaries secure the Phrygians
on the other side. No misery gnaws a free
man more than dishonor. Nature constrains
men more than chance. It is easy to be
a better archer with Teucer's bow. Wine-
stricken girls get drunker on eros. Who raises
goats where lightning strikes bushes? Mine
is a manner not swift-paced, but slow as horses
set free to graze. A wise man always looks
into books skeptically. Numbers are the chief
of sciences. When a storm blows, rogues, crooks
may take advantage, yet a rich man's a cleverer thief.
It is the mark of a just man to be angry at the gods
for life's calamity but not to honor them at all defies the odds.

A face's mirror is hard as bronze. The mind's mirror is wine.
Is it unseemly for the old to falter in wisdom?
If lamentation speaks in true measure, is it as fine
an expression of grief or sorrow as silence? Come
with me, Hermes, lord of games, play with me
in my house. Let us thrill to the rapture of mystic
hours. Before the portal of royal halls goes Hecate,
bearing her spells. With pomegranates, I like to pick
the bitter-sweet seeds and flick them on the floor.
Is it right that a fellow-traveller like me dance,
half-singing, half shouting, to the rites of Dionysos?
To know the strength of youth, to burn in its trance,
is to be deceived by time's consuming fires. If loss
is not a god it should be. Is that Charon knocking at my door?

2.

Fate laid-low these honorable spearman as they defended
their homeland, rich in sheep and goats. They were
steadfast in battle, clothed in the dust, the mud
of the field on which they fought, daringly, bravely,

against a great foe. Here lies what remains of the body
of Aeschylus, Athenian, Euphorion's son, who died in
the land of the wheat-bearing Geloans whose city
erected this tomb to proclaim his glory and valor at Marathon.

(After ancient Greek epitaphs)

Iphigenia Waves Goodbye as the Winds Pick Up on Aulis

He who pierced the heart of Artemis' deer is now
the killer of his daughter. Goddess, who
stilled the winds, why did you make him bow
to you in this way and not merely pursue
him yourself with your relentless bow and arrow

that never misses? I can hear the priests
from Chalcis sharpening their knives on stones
behind me, whetting them for me, the least
among my family and most innocent. Who hones
the ax, the murderous ax of destiny? Achilles

was never meant to marry me, destined to seize
Troy and die. So begins your war and with it history,
the children always the first to suffer and I am
that sacrifice, Agamemnon's daughter, my throat
to be slit not like a bull's or a ram's, but like a lamb's,

fresh from its mother's teat. I beg you. Look at me,
Father. See me clearly. Then go to your royal boat
and to your war, knowing my death is yours and, pitilessly,
all the world's you have doomed to endless catastrophes,
as I wave at you in the rising winds, resigned to die and bitterly happy.

(After the film by Cacoyannis)

The Lost Ghosts of Lemnos

I. The Play

1. Philoctetes:

Who are you? Why have you sailed to this
desolate place? Why have you harbored
your ship on this scarred rocky island? I miss
home. Why have you, heavily armed, labored

over harsh, crashing seas to lure me
out of my cave? I stink. I'm wounded,
hungry, alone. I want to die. I see
you smile. Why? Does the pain of others

amuse you? Am I a butt of your humor,
your jokes? I am wretched, despised
by those who long ago brought me here,
against all that's sacred. Why mock me further

with your silence? Does a man's suffering
bore or scare you more, the pus oozing
from my body? A venomous serpent
bit me. I've named it Terror, present

wherever warriors, heroes are. Where is home?
I lack food, clothes, friends. Take me
with you. I no longer live in sunlight,
but in a cave, wet and dark. You frighten

me with how you gaze at each other. Come,
save me, heal my wounds, end
my pain. This haunted island Lemnos
is peopled only by ghosts, living off loss.

2. *Chorus:*

We pity the man, but what can we do?
The pain he stuffers is our own.
We suffer also, we also
are exiles far from home.

Why must we be afraid of strangers,
be inconspicuous,
not look suspicious, risk the dangers
we face from those who disguise themselves as us?

Where do we dwell now, in what house,
habitat, homeland?
Where are the swallows, owls
hawks, bellowing bulls, sacrificial rams,

where the dancers with their laughter,
the nymphs of water,
nymphs of the meadows,
the south wind cooling us as it blows

through our valley? Now all is lost, for we,
though you can't see
us, live surrounded by
an imprisoning sea the gods say is eternity,

and yet we still dream of streams,
Lydian springs,
ripening olives. We are nothing
without our dreams

for they free us from Lemnos and the sea
around it. And we?
We are your unseen chorus,
the ghosts of your past within you. You'll never find us,

not even in the depths of caves soft breezes
flow through sweetly, bringing a sleep
so deep
it seizes us all, we who are doomed

to survive our deaths, missing
our lives, seeking
a way back or at least
a release

from time and the catastrophe
of never dying,
whether on earth or at sea
surviving in memories of a failed rejoicing.

3. *Philoctetes:*

You can't spare me from the war? Must I return to
my two-mouthed cave? Stripped
of all desire to live? To do
what? Wither away? Be repeatedly denied

sustenance, pleasures? I've become a one-winged
bird, a famished ram grubbing for grass
on a deserted island, nipping at dried
weeds to feed me, a cast-off refugee

from the fighting for which you need me
to win. Fiends. Monsters. Trespass
no more on my land with your injustices.
Why do you taunt me, tempt me? You ride

the seas as if you rule them, command the tide.
Your souls might reside inside your body
like spirits eager, longing to be free,
yet you intend to shackle me, to clamp me

in chains, steal my omnipotent bow. May you die
wounded and fetid as I am. Make
your libations, offer your sacrifices to rectify
your errors even as you tell me lie after lie.

All I have left now is my pride, Odysseus, and the power
of the bow you ask of me. No. I won't go
with you to Troy. Can't you hear my words echo
back at you from the mouth of my cave? No. No. No.

4. Chorus:

Let us sing to the seas,
to Poseidon,
earth shaker, tamer
of horses, savior of ships,

dark lord of the trident,
of his sixteen-hoofed chariot,
calmer
of turbulent

waters. May he bring peace
to us
and to Philoctetes.
Earth mother, nourisher,

life-bearer, dweller in mountains,
caves, plains,
in tombs and graves,
giver of grapes,

olives, flowers, fertile
fields, green hills,
wind-swept meadows,
gentle

rains, wife of the starry sky,
sister of the sea,
be
with us, comfort our grief

and Philoctetes' sorrow!
Okeanos,
and you, goddess of rebirth,
water, earth,

we tremble, cower
before your
power over
us.

We are the immortal ghosts
of Lemnos,
guardians over men's strife
and fears. Release

Philoctetes, us, his watchful chorus,
from our lives of sorrow.
Let us go home at last
to the joys you gave us so freely many years ago.

II. The Island

1. Lemnos

Lemnos is a small Greek island in the northern
Aegean Sea near the Hellespont and Gallipoli.
During The Great War allied foreign
troops were encamped there for the long
campaign against the Turks, who were militarily

superior, on the Dardanelles. It was wrong,
of course, to say so, but it was nonetheless
called another Trojan war. Three cemeteries

were dug there for the soldiers "slaughtered
like lambs," buried far from home, lost to memory.

Often fought over, then ignored, Lemnos is primarily
flat, like a desert, but the western part is rocky
and mountainous in places. There's one good
harbor and on the eastern shore a large bay.
The population numbers sixteen thousand today.

Summers, tourists crowd its beaches, eat Greek food
in the few modest bars or restaurants. Its weather
is Mediterranean, sunny and balmy, but occasionally
the winds blow so fiercely through valleys it's been
nicknamed the wind-ridden place. The surrounding sea,

crystalline and blue, is often calm, inviting swimmers in.
During Hellenic prehistory, it's thought, the women
of Lemnos, feeling deserted by their men for Thracian
girls, killed all the males remaining on the island,
an act deemed a Lemnian deed: "done cruelly, like a band

of barbarians." Many years ago, a necropolis
was discovered revealing bronze pots and an ossuary
containing funeral gifts, knives and axes
for the men; for the women, pins, necklaces, diadems
ornamented with gold spirals, suggesting Atreid origins.

2. *The Sacrifice*

On a nearby barren, smaller island, there
once stood an imposing altar to Philoctetes.
On it, a statue showed the hero wearing
a breastplate, holding a bow, and a brass
poisonous snake wrapped around each lower limb.

His wounds had been bandaged with strips of cloth.
But what did it depict on his face? Or say about him
or his war, the slaughter prolonged by the wrath
of Achilles? Suppose he had refused to go
to it, denying Odysseus', Neoptolemus', even Herakles'

entreaties and threats. Suppose he had kept his bow
against their insistence he give it to them,
instead retreating to his cave and its sorrows.
Would the desperate Greeks have pursued him,
killed him for his bow? Yes. But Philoctetes had quit the fight.

The Oracle had prophesied that no Greek could ignite
Troy on fire, ever win without his bow. I know
this is a fantasy, toppling history: Trojans rejoicing
as Greeks sail home, defeated; Aeneas denying
his destiny, staying home, never founding imperial Rome.

And yet even if his story is reimagined as a sacrifice
Philoctetes chose for peace, he would know, with sorrow,
he must stay in his cave forever out of the sight
of his fellow men, suffering, wondering at the price
of perpetual pain he'd paid to end humanity's suffering.

And so the lost ghosts of Lemnos recall to him, as if for
him alone, the Thessaly they'd shared, the place of their birth,
the plains, the vale of Tempe, Olympus, the rugged shore
along the Aegean, the summer rains renewing the winter's earth,
the Pineios flowing from the Pindus Range into a strange, unknown sea.

III. Choral Song

Strophe

> The gods are often vengeful
> but bless us, too, though
> none can evade the toll
> of tears and pain we know
> throughout our lives.
> But this is a song for lovely
> Agido, leader of the chorus.
> Bliss it is to hear her, dazzling
> to look upon her, Pegasus-
> like, dream-like, swift
> and winged, her face pale,

radiant as silver. Twirl, lift
your skirts, dance, dance for us,
Agido, leader of the chorus.

Prance through the agora,
oh, lovely Hagesichora.
Each glance you cast us
saves us. See how she
blooms into gold, bearer
of joy, blazing bright
as a star. And here are
Aphrodite and her child,
wild Eros, running through
flowers, untouchable
flowers belonging to the gods'
empyrean meadows where
every singer, with her melodies
and praises, longs for us to follow them.

2. *Antistrophe*

Neither luxurious purple dye,
snake-eyed coral bracelets,
cloth sheer as butterfly's
wings, nor the sun as it sets
over iris-blue waters
can please the gods more
than Agido or Nanno or Thulakis
with their immortal beauty.
Song, only song, song alone
survives all hopes. Gods, accept
our prayers. May no one sing
in vain who has kept true
to their vows to art. Sparrows are
trilling, sweetly calling us from rooftops.

Listen. The earth's music is like sea-birds
at twilight skimming the surface of waves
birthing fresh flowers of light
like the Pleiades at night unfurling
in the sky, scattering its petals,
while dusk's fierce Scythian horses
are hauling Orthria's harvest cart
toward heaven in pursuit of sleep
in deepest obscurity. Ladies of dawn,
come nearer. Heal us of our cares
and troubles. Relieve our fears. Bring
us peace, Agido, you who sing
like a swan by the river Xanthos while
you toss, twirl your youthfully free, tawny hair.

3. Epode

Voices, sweetly calling, ancient voices, alluring music,
take me, carry me, sick at heart, with you.
To free us from the world's iron grip only your lyre,
your art suffices, Agido. Dance on. Aspire
to survive even as centuries pass. There are
no furies, no sirens to fear now, no gods to serve
slavishly. Chorus leader, solitary singer, preserve
the rites. Hear me. You know what I want. You
see who I am, what I've become. None can bear
my limbs up from earth now. Allow me to follow
you, to join you in song. Commend my performance.
All ships must at last sail to a final port. All chariots
must race to the pace of the trace horse. What's done
is never undone, sung never unsung. Change fate, betray me.

(After Sophocles and Alcman)

Andromache and Astyanax Wait for Death on the Palace's Parapet

My dear son, you must be killed, my beloved
boy, my only son, Hector's, mine,
savaged, ravaged until you're dead,
freed from pain, Priam's royal line
ended as my agony, like none other,

begins, a doomed mother unshielded
by soldiers, married more to slaughter
than my lost husband. My child, boy,
why do you weep, pull at my dress,
like a hungry orphan in great distress

seeking succor from a passing stranger?
Your father and I made you for joy
not this suffering, this ruin. Embrace
me. Let me feel your sweet, warm breath
on my body one last time, here on my breast

where I nursed you. Kiss me, my lips. Place
your hands on my shoulders. Try to rest
in my arms. You and I will wait for death
to come to us together, here on this parapet
as Troy burns and bleeds around us. Why

should we want to live longer, Astyanax? Let
us be brave as your father. There's a fatality
men call history, my son. Helpless, I look
down at the rocks you'll be cast upon, with me
to follow as I leap over this wall to join you,

our broken bodies' blood flowing together the sole clue
others must pursue if they're to understand
why the unity of a mother and her child, begun
in the womb, is unending, that no cruel hand
can take that from her: this lie that I've died with my son.

(After Euripides)

20

Patroclus at the Edge of the Earth

Avernus, beyond its cavernous clammy depths,
seizes us, embraces us, unworthy of its darker
mysteries. The mark of a good man, just
and wise even in calamities, is never
to succumb to anger, is a noble man
never provoked to wrath by words or deeds.
But our world knew better: that fury is god-
given like a divinity-driven howl of misery
at the end of a tragedy, raging against fate's duplicities.

Here, waiting at earth's edge, squinting, I see,
rising toward the heavens, a missive flame,
like lightning flashing skyward, or eyes alight
with desire, burning from longing for the war
to be over. From northlands, a blackly violent
wind chills my heart, icier than in winter.
It is what men once meant by fate: the silent,
insidious welding of brute force and its power,
like the blessings revoked from this desolate land.

Is the present more just than the past? We're all
of the mortal sort, share one destiny.
Why else do we abandon hope, grow into
hovering, smoky shadows, like memory
I'm told, while it waits for blood to drink
to tell wanderers who chance upon it its story,
flickering like a solitary candle in a damp, dank cave.

Is a shade's life's recurrent dying akin to
being born twice? Alive, I thrilled to Eros'
rites when with Achilles. What a pair we
made, none stronger, none more free,
more rapturous than we were, he
with his marble beauty, flowing hair,
I with the scents of nard and balsam
on my tongue from the perfumes his sweat
wore, tasting of pomegranates and sweet berries.

21

Our lightning-smitten bodies trembled
during fucking's storms, the thunder-
bolts we scattered behind us stirring winds,
waking dogs, howling back at its power,
our cocks after like two limp swords
we'd abandoned, bent and useless,
that in our exhaustion we'd consigned
to dust as if passion were a battle field
whose fairest flowers had all been taken
by armed hosts, defeating us ignobly,
returning to their wives, children, hearths
safely behind their city's gates and battlements,
a city rumored to have been glorious once,
and, like all things great, most favored by
the gods, while we slept in our tents dreaming
of ships and home, fathers, brothers left in peace.

The holy mute heavens, the Olympian deaf ones
wound the earth because they can.
Where in the West now is the bowl wrought
by Hephaestus, the urn of sovereignty,
the artful order from which the living drink
as if from a mighty river that girds the earth
while flowing freely from the gloom below
it even to the world's furthest reaches where
I stand, the sun's golden wine jug denied
us shades who must not sip of it nor know
any comfort, blinded by dead men's night-
time follies, excesses of memory, incapacity
to lament, to mourn like the living, never
to know again dawn's bright flashes, its torches'
bearing glory to the commands of Apollo
and his boyfriend, wine-stricken, incessantly
rising again, ever surprising, drunk, aflame with love.

(After scattered fragments from Aeschylus)

The Twice-Born God Arrives in Hellas

Whisper these fragments as if they were secrets
uttered to bring down kingdoms. For the house
is maddened by a god. Beneath its palaces'
roofs, men revel with his drunken frenzy, wearing
Lydian tunics and fox-skin cloaks like women's
dresses down to their sandals. Who in the world,
the foolish insist, is this mad prophetic poet,
this woman-man? What besotted land does he
come from, long-legged, robed, and uncastrated,
tumultuously phallic? And the women, the women
rise, woken, to his cymbals. clanging, the pounding
drums as if aroused by him into the wilderness
of their unfettered passions, miming the bull-
voiced bellows of Hades' thunder, inspiring terror,
the unmasked power of his bronzed body's revelations
like the sharp, deadly scorching of his breath on your body.

Oh, Zeus, father Zeus, you are air, you are earth,
you are all things and the joy that transcends
them. Teach your daughters in your new ways
of mourning. And for your sons, let gush
more abundant springs. We dwell under
the bowl of your sky near a mighty river
that girds the wide earth. Let us flee night
on your holy steeds. Send them to us
with all due speed so that we may hear
the oracles that you, Father Zeus, have
given to Loxias: that our great kingdom
might not fall to rioters and transgressors
of your laws as we offer to you blessings,
true libations. Zeus, our mind's unblinded savior, spare
us, save us from your dainty-stepped bird, coiled-
snake, twice-born, dark-eyed mistake of a child. Come. Heal us.

(After scattered fragments from Aeschylus and Euripides' Bacchae)

II.

Hortations

1. *To a Randy Old Man*

Foolish old boyfriend of sad old Ibycus,
it's long past time for you to quit
your promiscuous ways. Be honest
with yourself. You're no longer young,
far closer to death. Stop acting
like a boy cruising parks in too
tight jeans and t-shirts, devoting
nights to Grindr. What's right for
youth is wrong for you. Trust me.

You're like a cloud in the sky obscuring
stars, a thumb on the lens of a camera.
You act as if you were handsome
still, but you're not. You're wrinkled
and bald. Why do you think you can
lay siege to boys in bars as if you
were Bacchus plying with wine a kid
whose face makes your heart beat
like a drum, lubricious as a cat in heat?

Dear old man, you'd be better off
knitting a wool sweater against
winter cold than trying another
binge diet to slim down. Listen
to the music of a lyre playing in
a room filled with blooming fresh
red roses recalling how you emptied
wine-jars at evening revels long ago,
if you must. Then head to bed with sweaty Ibycus.

(After Horace 3.15

2. *To a Beautifully Cruel Boy*

Dear cruel boy, so finely endowed with
a divine beauty offered you by
Apollo: looking good as you
know you do, be advised. The day
will come faster than you think
when you'll stare at the mirror,
finding there, unbelievably, wrinkled
skin, a bald scalp in place of your
blond locks and rosy-hued complexion.

"Alas," you'll say. "Heu, heu, for what
I was before. If only I knew then
what I know now, I would not
have been cruel to you and you or you
as beautiful boys will dis me now.
I blame Apollo, for what do gods
know of time and sorrow to those
they endow with their favor only
to watch their beauty go long before they die?"

Be merciful when you can be young,
then. Learn to act kind early. You'll
not be yourself to yourself soon,
it's true: fair hair no more brushing
your shoulders, blushing cheeks
gray and pale, dewy lips cracked
and dry. Just yesterday, you were
glorious. Tomorrow, who knows how
you'll survive. But you do, you will, dear baby boy.

(After Horace 4.10)

3. *To a Boy New to Love*

Suppose this were you. (I admit
it's a sad situation.) You've yet
to become a player in the game
of love. You're an erotic neophyte.
Who isn't at some time under
the thumb of someone censorious,
parent, friend, the law? You cannot
take even a taste of the weakest
wine or the pleasures of dirty books.

Venus is unknown to you, engaged
as you are in your devotions
to duty and the household gods,
one of whom seems to have run
off with several of your sketches.
Then one day, at the river, you catch
sight of Septimius swimming in it,
the sun glowing off his shoulders
while your soul overflows with his splendor.

You hear he's a better rider than
Bellerophon ever was, an undefeated
boxer, a heralded runner, that he
flees as fast as wild-eyed stags,
flies higher than hawks: you're in love,
for the first time, and you've become
its wingèd child concealed in a dark
thicket by the rushing Tiber day after day,
like a boar in hiding, not afraid, waiting, hard for his arrow.

(After Horace 3.12)

Aesthetics

1.

Haughty Ligurinus, unhappy in your sensuous,
enticing, painful cruelty. Flirty, vain Ligurinus,
your beauty, it's been said by your lovers,
is what brought them the joy each suffers

from the lack of, now that you're out of their lives,
a joy that, in memory at least, strangely survives
your absence. For your face's become beard-
heavy with bristling whiskers, your lovelier-than-even-

Apollo-could-endure rose-colored cheeks, I've heard,
have faded. I fear for you. Old age is a burden
we all must bear or die young. Who today offers
you silver or gold jewels for the pleasures of your company?

2.

A rose grows lovely only to be picked first and so to die.
Tomorrow tragedy awaits. The loveliest in our garden,
you chase after a blond, buffed Eros half your age. Don't
deny it, Ligurinus. Even now you lie and lie and lie

to yourself each time you embrace him or look in a mirror.
O, my dear, try to forget how cruel you've been for
so long, a stone cold statue. Now you burn for a boy
who's thrice refused a silver ring he called a crackerjack toy.

No, no, Ligurinus. None of us feels any satisfaction
in this turn of events. We mourn for you, the vanity
of our folly as well as yours. Youth, the gods abandon
us all. Honor, while you can, your beauty by giving it generously.

(After Horace 4.10 and 1.36)

30

Wise Advice

Offer devotion to the gods, even if you
don't believe in them. You can't be
too careful, can you? If it's true
or not will not matter. Freely
praise them. It's like practical politics,
shifting a ship's course on stormy
seas, changing horses midstream.
Or following both epicureans and stoics
to avoid any offense. Who you seem
to be is all people need attend to.
So be it. Truth is famously elusive and blurry.

Or be an atheist if you prefer. But Jupiter
rides in a thundering chariot
and is said to shatter
men with one bolt, one shot
of his arrow, willy nilly, you might
say. One day, a friend went fishing.
Before he had time to fight
a huge bass on his line he was plunging
into the Styx. Who know why?
Maybe he was drunk, maybe just high.
You see, Boy? Life entails considerable danger.

For just in the merest wink of an eye,
with a flick of a god's finger,
you might be hurled deathward. Try
to understand. Dying never
makes a lick of sense. Shadowlands,
empyrean heights, either way the odds
are set against us. Dip your hands
in warm bull's blood to please the gods.
Why risk sickness or more needless distress?
Practice prayer. Chant hymns. Or mess
with magic. But never do anything too risky.

Life is a trick too hard to bring off.
Pray, if you must, even to a dictator.
"Hear me, do not mock me, scoff
at me, my divine Emperor
Augustus," you wisely say
to save your skin, with fervor
if possible. "I am a man, nothing
more." And with a little luck,
birds of fortune might soon be flapping
their wings above you, as if they give a fuck
about what happens to you, now or in the future.

(After Horace 1, 34)

Monsters

Day trudges after day, moons rise and fall,
as a man of fabled wealth ponders
his mortality, when death might call
him, he to have no choice in the matter,
a proud man and, it's true, a greedy
s.o.b. Why shouldn't he build another
empty mansion, a pricier, huge, gaudy
shrine to himself? He's been told it's never
too late to be kind, good, even charitable,
but so what? He loves wealth far more
than people. And the pain he's caused? Don't be
silly. Men are wolves to men. Morality's simple.
Build higher walls. Electrify the gates. Lock every door.
The poor are not your problem, only their numbers.

So enjoy, gloat over your resplendent excesses,
What else is life good for but show? Be proud
of the pitiless rents, the exorbitant fees
you demand of renters, borrowers, that crowd
of the impoverished in their miserable
hovels, huts, lugging their few belongings
away in cardboard boxes, loosely bound
with plastic wraps while holding the intolerable,
callused hands of their children and doddering,
arthritic parents. So what if the land you kick
them off was once theirs? Woeful, bleeding
hearts claim what you do is worse than theft. Lick
his ass, you losers. So what if you cast them out
with nowhere to go? Power over others is what life's about.

Should you be grateful for the gifts you were given
the occasional welcome meal, feast, booze,
the help a few offered to ease and hasten
your climb up the ladder? But didn't you choose
your own way, never one to be content
with impoverishment, your outcast father's
harsh existence, a man who left no monument
behind him, no sign that he had ever
existed? When it's over no one knows what
any life has meant. Modest things, common
pleasures, longings were not what you were cut-
out for, only easy girls, silver chalices, Illyrian wine,
golden barges cruising down wide ambling rivers
might satisfy you. Boasting of them, you should say, "I've won."

Boring men advise you, "Darkest Orcus is eternally
eager to greet wicked folks like you into his infernal
halls, old man. You're ill now, worrisomely
so. You know how death is eager to haul
you underground. Yet you buy more
and more, inflicting your vile will upon
the sick and impoverished. Cruel Tantalus,
vengeful Medea, proud Prometheus, tyrannical
Sisyphus are imprisoned forever together. You've won?
Charon never tires of taunting those whose ruinous
lives have destroyed others." To which you reply, easily,
"Death is death, that nothing, when each of us dies,
we must become." So why be good? The trick is to stick
to your guns, delaying oblivion so it comes later, painless and quick.

(After Horace 2, 18)

34

A Riposte to Horace

1.

Wise people scatter from mad poets,
run away fast, afraid to touch them
like rabid dogs or folks affected with
communicable diseases. You know
whom I mean: the ones even little
children mock and scorn when they
hear them recite their babbling verses,
staring wildly up at the sky as if seeking
inspiration from wingless birds falling
from heaven or pondering the depths
of wells they might fall into in the midst
of drunken frenzies. Say it happens.

"Help," he cries. "Friends, save me."
So one wonders, maybe he doesn't
really want to be helped. And another
proposes he fell into it at his own free
will. It's possible. After all, the Sicilian
poet, Empedocles, leapt into a volcano
volitionally. Poets do kill themselves
sometimes. Perhaps this one wanted
to also, not the first to fall down
a well. What I mean to say is when you
listen to poets you're never sure if they
are sensible people. And a few do give
up their lives to make a notorious death.

Why are poets poets anyway? I heard
one recently brag he'd pissed on his
father's ashes. Another boasted he'd
committed sacrilege on a holy place.
And another, the craziest, vowed to fight
anyone he met who'd booed him during
his dreadful readings. He was like a bear
that had broken out of his cage or a leech

35

sucking his listener's blood.. So you
understand, my friend, why I ask you
dearly in an era of so many lunatics,
what makes you think poets write sanely?

2.

Yes. Let poets give us new names for things.
Let them make language richer. In forests,
fresh leaves signal the changing year.
The old ones drop away; the new ones come
and bloom and prosper in their due time.
We're all bound to die and join them in earth.
Men make bays, docks, harbors to shelter
fleets from storms. Swamps confuse us,
tangle oars, impossible to sail on. We plow
the earth to nourish ourselves, raise river
banks to save our seeded fields from flooding.
All things that mortals do are fatal and our
glory, duly measured to the music and beat
of our lives in their formal, orderly beauty,
is like yours, my friend, who loved the language
of Homer and Archilochus and our great Virgil,
yet would not write a word, mindful, afraid
of the fashionable ways of those who'd piss on
the ashes of tradition and subject others to their
derisions, with a madness, a rage no poetry can
cure. Instead I offer my silence, the empty page,
the forgotten days of a poet no one will remember.

III.

Goodbye to My Friend

In May, a southern wind sifts through barley
fields grown nutty and golden. Jujube
flowers, grasshopper green, the green
of ivy, have not yet fallen.

Clusters of Seven-Son Flowers, pungent
and lustrous., are about to blossom
into their white luminescence, turned
bright pinkish-red in autumn.

Remember how we parted in the green
mountains, how our horses whinnied
on the way, eager to return home,
to life as it was before?

Dear friend, in life you stood stalwart
and tall, your beard long as a dragon's,
eyebrows like those of a tiger,
forehead massive as a buddha's,

while your mind stored the wisdom of ten
thousand books, never to bow
to flatterers or mediocrity.
How I miss those days.

The day we met, we got drunk at the Temple
Gate, happy, light-hearted as we
basked in the sun, gazing at clouds
drifting as we drifted and as lonely.

Now the river near me floods mercilessly,
surging on shore late into night.
In the morning, a ferryman checks
his boat, too battered to sail.

Travelers from Henan have not yet gone.
Travelers to Luoyang sigh wistfully.
Long ago, I heard of your days
in the forest, through with your labors.

And so you died while generations passed
between us as if beyond time.
And I do not know what my life means
anymore, nor what I should do tomorrow.

    (After Li Qi)

In a Time of the Breaking of Nations

1.

Sometimes love is about coming together,
sometimes it's about separating, even
a love between you and your country.

The moon's light slants acutely on the roofs
of a nation. Wave farewell to it.
In the aftermath of last night's rain,

beneath the haze of a lunar halo, a raccoon
sloshes through withered grass sniffing
for food like you hunting for all you'd thrown away.

2.

When a country fails, it leaves no
footprints in the snow, none
in the sand, no marks on carpets.

We are two ghosts of the heart,
you and I, fellow citizens
of what used to be, journeying,

summoning cries which no one can hear
over the harsh winds blown
off the sea, wetting our faces, heavy as tears.

3.

Resist, we're told, as the curtain of the night
folds and unfolds. The place where
we used to rest is called the House

of the Never Grieve. Sleepless, we assure
each other that a love of nation
is not folly, then look out the window

where the laws of night, crowned by darkness,
yield to dawn no pity even as its wings
try to flame back to life.

4.

If, dear friends, you come to regret leaving
later, you'll be like a ship sailing
toward a foreign harbor,

watching driftwood floating this way,
that way on a choppy sea,
gazing wistfully toward the land

you unwillingly abandoned, while all around
you scales of tiny feeding fishes
glitter obscenely, ecstatically.

5.

How long does it take for a passion
to become a distant memory,
a lost country? Stars mark

its maps of desolation, the fading horizon
between life and death.
Goodbye, goodbye. The park is full

of locusts and twilight, like philosophers trying
to find reasons for why a state has died,
like a work of art, obdurate in its obscurity.

6.

I should be glad should this loss become
only a hunted memory. Wind, dew,
a calm clear morning.

Whose February is this? If I could force passion
into sentience, would I? To weep,
to laugh: aren't the two

indistinguishable? Shimmering clouds,
rolling waves, both merciless
to the one exiled within himself, inside his locked city.

7.

Distant letters, dreams of reconciling, of returning to
how it used to be. All we have now are empty
beds, depleted shelves, unfurnished rooms,

and a winter rain filled with an anguish that means
to cry this cry: Oh. beauteous
world, embrace the sun, the dawn tenderly,

its light like a lover's skin silken and tensile.
If we ever meet each other again,
will we know who we are or who we were then?

8.

I ask you when you think you'll be back. You reply,
There is no when. If I should shout out
my fears intemperately, how many heads

would turn as one to heaven or a clearer sky?
Hear it? It's like the voices of a better
world pleading for us to change our fear of abandonment

into another's redemption. Tomorrow, tomorrow, ever,
ever, we say, while our.country is like wild horses running
toward precipitous hills, faster, faster, rampaging earth without us.

(After Li Shangyin)

A Rainy Morning

1.

Few are the days of spring when we are old,
the rain cold when it should be warm. How
unbearably happy our lives might have been,

no matter the too many times I have had
to say it. I had to leave you far behind,
so far the earth broke apart between us.

The ivy's jade-sleek leaves are flourishing.
(Speak of this to no one, not even in dreams.)
The roses' petals look brittle as crystal bowls.

(No hope is endless as waves in an ocean.)
The damp ruins my books piled in boxes,
the letters you sent me. A man alone knows

his spirit is always at odds with the season,
his words a long sickness weakening his body,
his thoughts like seeds withering, randomly scattering.

2.

Sometimes I fear what light I see will not
survive the night, yet a too bright sun
burns my mind to ashes. So I rise

and decline by the moon. Where is the Pure Land,
its sure Radiance? Today, the rain falls
so gently it weaves itself into lace brocades

shimmering in the wind. (How beautiful
is nature's kindness sometimes.) My body's
become a winter field a late snow refuses

to melt from even while trees are greening,
my hair's no longer golden as sands by the sea
but white as strands of twine. (How beautiful,

yet foolish.) The night I left, I could not look back
toward the darknesss into which you were fading
as day broke suddenly, brightening the abyss between us.

3.

Even my pillow will not talk, even my bed
will not confess to spring. White cloth
means white troubles, regret's emptiness

the belatedness of sorrow. I want to see
you, I want to be by you as in a mirror.
If there were a next world, I would meet

you there, hold you in my arms. White dew
means white illusions. Love has no color.
The rain on the oak leaves has turned into

mist. (Why must the body fail to follow
its heart's desires?) I've walked wooded
paths where ghostly friends rush to greet me.

(What took you so long?, they ask). The place
where I live lacks pure souls. I miss your voice,
the way you talked to me, the way spring used to be.

(After Sugawara No Michizane, Lady Ise, and Lady Izumi)

Hawks' Flight

1.

My love left the house. I could
not stop him. Which road did
he take? Which way would he
follow? I have no spirit now.

And this is all there is, just this.
We counted on ten thousand years.
All we possess are our broken bodies.
We live in a world that fades with no traces.

When I reach out to touch him, I touch
nothing. We meet each night in dreams.
As I pass by the ford where plovers,
feed in the river bed, I hear his cry.

It is painful to meet in dreams. Snow
falls in a foreign sky whose
mountains are too high to climb.
My hawk leaves my arms, returns with no effort.

Or it flies on and on, lost in clouds,
its invisibility a fire burning in
my brain, an ice-sheet melting
on the shrine to the island's gods—

my love's vowing to come back to me
like an arrow-tailed hawk perched
on me whose keen talons gripped
my gloved arm, eyes wild, beak bloodied.

2.

Spring comes as the last light of
night wanes into silence. A robin
beats its wing and cries. What
fallow field does it call its home?

Willows trail my steps wherever
I go, walk with me in sorrow.
At the temple well, I draw water,
drink, tasting dew on violets, pine twigs.

It is the season for swallows to
appear, for wild geese to fly over
in destitution, recalling their lost
nests in the red-leafed mountains.

Daybreak is mournful to look at,
the mists, the boatmen hazy, far
away, two young girls singing
as they pole a boat on an unchanging river,

flowing as it flowed before time began,
their faces' red glow fading, their hair
black as flowers' seeds. Even the trees
speak no words. Even my heart is silent.

I'd like to spend what remains of my life
where reed leaves blow in gentle breezes
as I stare at the sky whose vastness composes
its passing songs to the alone and slowly dying.

(After Otomo No Yakamochi)

A Pine Tree Backdrop

When I was still in the world, spring was always
beside me. I feasted with the spirits
of clouds, shared flowers with them. My days
knew no self-pity. Maple leaves. Sprigs
of cherry blossoms. Artful pine. The moon
was my mirror, a night-enfolded morning-
glory. Life ends too late or too soon.
I grow envious of your sorrow, yet yearn
for my grief to subside, return to its possessor.
My body has no roots, fades like dew from leaves.
So long as it lasted, we stayed true to one another.
Who is it who pursues my heart, mourns, grieves
with me, friends, lovers with the forbearance of holy things,
the flash of fireflies in the dark, deities like trees bending to winds?

(After the ghost in Pound's version of Awoi No Uye)

Ghosts

1. Kudzu

In rain, warm rain, seek the undifferentiated
things of the teachings, the transient world.
The law spares neither grass nor tree. All bend
to the wind. Waves rise and fall, hurled
this way, that. Even after death, we suffer,
shed tears on the vines that bind themselves
to pine and red maple, flow like water over
forest floors. Who tells stars' stories tells
us all. We lose our beauty by weeping, meet
thereafter only by night where the vines, holy
vines slither over us, wrap round us, greet
us in the earth where we lay by day, invisible
to the ghosts of our hearts, the moon still able
to see us, like evening rains, torrential floods of reality.

(After passages in the Noh play Teika)

2. War

Temples with their thousand pines. Civil wars.
Soldiers' camps. My thoughts are stacks of
bundled grass, pillows of stone. Murmurs
of peace sussurate through weeds, fallow
fields, my fellows' tents, caked with snow.
What good is music offered to the gods now,
to chant in the Buddha's name from love
for one's ghosts? Year after year adds up to
only more sitting by the stove, roasting
potatoes. Yellow leaves are my gold, blue
feathers my sapphires. Come, friends, blow
my lamp out with me. Rain falls from eaves
onto my writing paper. Who stays, who leaves?
Forty years and nothing but this, this waiting for peace.

(After passages by Taikyoku Zosu and Keijo Shurin)

49

3. *Travelers in a Storm*

Storms force trees to yield their leaves. Who will
show them the way? The land is pitted
with showers, the grass drenched. A still,
lone shadow in the form of a mountain
rests under clouds, the gray, unsettled
sky. A fox cries out from ivies they've lain
on like a bed, two lone travelers roaming hills,
far from their birthplaces. Night falls. They
find a cave to sleep in where there's a dream-
bridge over a rushing river. Where might they stay
for the rest of their days, the past lately flooded,
fast vanishing upstream, the river's weight heaped
high on ghosts voyaging to autumn's reddening to gold.
They hike temple-bound till gate-side, ring the bell as they'd been told.

(After passages in Nishikigi in Pound's version)

The End of an Affair

1.

Sometimes desire, while it sleeps,
wanders through night like a river

flowing in the dark where it drifts
until morning when a breeze ripples

its surface as it curves eastward,
toward day. Warm as spring rain,

first light washes over your body
like a Matisse, painting it the color

of the amber flecks sparkling in your
irises, the golden-red dawn of your hair.

2.

A man trying to be wise or a man
struggling to be good might end

the same way, no matter how
or why, like wolf's teeth or snake

skin drying under an indifferent sky.
Might a sensuous man relish

life more than a chaste one?
It's spring. Apple blossom petals

twist in the breeze as they fall.
In the silence between us, we can hear

the dew dripping off the lip-like red tips
of roses, the limbs and cones of pine trees.

3.

How to explain your tears at the ringing
of the chapel's bells as it broke

the moonlight's silence? Did you feel
loosed from earth, freed from time?

The wind whistling past our windows,
crows waking, cawing, flying off

their scraggly perches, winged-seeds
twisting in the air, dust clouds

rushing across an empty street: what
about their mingled music made you weep?

4.

Your crying eyes left nothing
for my sight to bind to, the bright

bravery of things lately blinded,
an early May morning reborn

in the mirror reflecting you more
clearly in the ease of your departure.

You stood by our bed like a brother,
naked, turning away, like a shadow

struggling to reawaken without
speaking, quiet as a silkscreen

we'd seen of a mourner, bent over
from grief, making his way to a shrine by the river.

(After Li Ho)

IV

Conundrums

1.

Abandoned before birth by my begetters,
I was still dead the first day of spring.
No heart beats in my breast, no flutters
in my chest, no signs of my breathing.

I was clothed in what a kinswoman had worn,
but kinder than my blood, who swaddled,
comforted me as if I'd been her own new born.
In time, I grew great with life, fostered

by her who nursed me, fed me till I had grown
big enough to set my sights further, far
away, though she was heard to moan
loudly for the child she never had, I not her son or daughter.

2.

As long as my ghost lives, I walk on my own two
feet, shaking the ground and wide meadows.
I bind the hands of black-haired strangers and a few
much superior, yet I am one who's known true sorrows.

I might be a vessel for men to drink from my belly.
A bride once set her foot on me.

Far from the west, a dark-haired girl grabs
me, hugs me, a drunken fool,
washes me with water like other lads
she gets wet for, uses me like a tool
for her pleasure. She squeezes me between
her breasts with her hot hand and leans
over me as I lick her nether part. Name

me if you can, who live much the same
as you, off the yield of the land,
and fertile dead, laboring for what others have stolen
like contraband.

3.

I am fire-ecstatic, possessed like wood.
I am light. Flames lap my body.
I bear the strength of storms. Should
I need to, I can manage to fly.
I am a stand of trees, leaf-bearing,
ruddy as embers. Who am I?

From friend to friend, I roam
round the hall, lords and ladies
eager to kiss me. When I hold myself high,
look how the whole company
grows silent before me. Oh, seize
the day while you can for its blessedness,
as I flourish skyward, no more, no less
than your unknown shadow. Who am I when not at home?

4.

I watched a man with his exposed, weaponized
cock stalk me until, aflame with primary,
unbounded lusts he seduced me, forced
me to succumb, shooting into me,
the fountain of his youth.

Who dares to ask, What is truth?
Another man, standing near us, asked
me, "What beast is he who, living, will break
souls into clods of dirt, take
away their virtue, destroy their integrity,
bind their hands, tie
their lives into knots, never to understand why,
not what of youthful ruth
is yours, my Lord, but what of our sorrows yet to be?"

5.

I heard and saw a wonder. Moth-, fly-eaten words.
A man's poetry swallowed by
worms. Its serpent-bound sentences
like the sounds of snorting pigs, herds
of cattle. Someone is standing bedside. Try
to imagine it. How fear sometimes pleases
me. A robber-guest who rustles past me in the night.
And I, for all the fright I felt at his sight,
felt none the wiser for it, for the words he mumbled
so weirdly. Who was he, and why do I feel so unsatisfied
when he fails to return to me or dies at the morning light?

6.

Wave after wave, the fated, hated thing
I saw, finely wrought, wonderfully ornate,
riding like a ship at sea, a wonder surmounting
wave upon wave: the water, for which I wait,
white as bone, as dead flesh is, wildly free and freeing.

7.

Home is not a silent place. Nor am I loud.
The Lord provides for us both, a voyage
which we share. I'll do what is allowed,
no more. Occasionally I turn the page
of a book faster than he does, am speedier,
read faster, discover how it ends, no passage
skipped, before he does. Or I am a runner
running faster than he attempts? Yet, for as long
as I live I live in him, his way is mine, his song
is my song. But if we should separate, be partners
no more, he will live after me and I will die. Why is this not wrong?

8.

God is
good,
omniscent,
omnipotent.
It's simple.
Solve
this hoary puzzle
for evil.

9.

Many men met together, discrete men,
wise and witty, and then
another walked in. Who?

Was it you?
Two ears, but only
one eye.

Two feet, but twelve hundred
heads. Bent back,
fat belly, a stack

of hands but just
two sides,
ams, shoulders, one

neck, as normal.
Who said
life holds no surprises?

Giant-sized, tall,
lust-
ful. Name him, please.

10.

I feed in the depths of the sea, close
to land. Often, in the ocean,
I open my mouth. Who knows
why I have no feet? What reason
is there for me to be meat for man
whose knives are always sharp enough
to slice me up? Though my hide's tough,
he devours me raw, eats me uncooked because he can,
season after season. Tell me, friend, what call you then
this devotion?

(After the Exeter Riddles)

Vanitas

Well-hewn tall stone walls fate-shivered
to pieces, the Great Hall fallen...beams
split, towers riven.
                    Giants worked
them, stone-smithies, now mould-, rime-
smitten, rime on gates, crumbled mortar,
shield-shaped roofs shattered.
                              Who
wielded, wrought them are gone, grasped by,
grave-snatched by earth...fathers, sons,
numbering fifty...more...lichen on walls,
wine-colored stones where kings clashed
and fell, hacked, ground down...passed into
earth, sinking, crusted with loam, laden
with clay.
          Still bound fast with iron the old walls'
 bases, a woeful wonder.
                        Springs ran through
the halls, thronged, clattering with noise,
sounds of the mead-drunk, gables helmeted
with war-horns.

          Wild fate ruins all...days
of great sickness...death catching up
to, snatching men...battlefields wasted...
rebuilders shrunken to, re-taken by earth,
arches twisted to broken tiles, roofs riven,
doomed downward.
                Once many a glad, good
man stood there, heightened, brightened
by gold, ruddy with drink, his war-gear donned,
gazing upon gems, amber, silver, gold,
bought, hoarded, yet weirdly wrought.
                                      Once

many a stone house stood where warm
waters sprang from their sources, the baths
hot as hearth embers...whence steaming
streams flowed over hoar-frosted rocks into
ring-shaped pits hewn from rough gray stone.

                      Ruined now, all lost
now, gone, death-fated, doomed.

                       It is a kingly thing...
aetheling...pride...pryde...an earthly city....

you, yours....

    (After The Ruins)

Desire's Gold-Hoards

1.

Watch a strong man stretch a long bow. Be
that powerful. Observe how a flame
burns. Be that patient. When you see
a wolf show its teeth, a bear do the same,

learn what bravery means. A fat grunting pig's
worth more than a rootless tree, a rising wave
more than a boiling kettle. A homeless man digs
his own grave gladly. An icy night spent in a cave

with a coiled snake his only companion tests
a man's mettle more than a warrior's boasting
of his prowess. A woman's bed-talk, denying rest,
is like a broken sword, useless in battle. Behaving

like a child playing fools no one. A seer who foretells
only good is as risky to face as an unburied
body. Never trust either, nor unsown fields nor wells
run dry. A man is only as wise as his capacity for hatred.

2.

Back have I turned, believing I was going to love,
back from certain pleasure, back from shame
altogether, back from disdain, the battles above,
the carnage below, my incessant search for fame.

So I came here, long afterwards, standing ready
where soul-fighters lie awake all night, holding
burning brands in their hands, demanding to carry me
where hoarded gold leads onward toward nothing

but grief and loss while the flames inside me are burning
to return to that love-sick Great Hall I attacked once
and have come back from, back to the good thing
silence is, the ineloquent language of a man who hunts

62

for his lust's prey like wolves in the forest of memory
with no laws or wise men to warn of the perilous way,
transient, irresistible as autumn nights, high waves at sea,
or Northern winds roaring though woods on a scorching summer day.

(After Sayings of the High One)

A Journey to the Land of the Dead

Saddle-laid, to the far dark world he rode
where he faced a hell-hound, its breast
dripping with blood, barking, as it told
of dire, foreboding things while the rest
of time broke over him like the crest
of a wave. Then he reached the eastern
gate and the horary seer of all that is,
chanting her spells to the fallen and broken,
that they, newly dead, rise out of the mist,
the men that sat on the benches of the mead
halls, though here a shield lay over their golden
brew, the many brave sons despairing from need
of that fortifying drink, waiting for her to speak
of whatever mystery it is that the living need to seek

answers to, the knowledge of death. "One night old,
though not long away, your brother Vali will slay you,
neither cleanse your hands, nor comb your gold
hair." "Say more, seeress," he insists. "Why pursue
what you oughtn't to know?," she replies. "Who
are the women who will greet me some day
with the corners of their kerchiefs heaved to the sky?"
"Not headdresses but the sails of the ship where you lay
being carried to sea to be set on fire where all will die
with you in that wave-borne blaze of the finest ship
ever built, Hringhorni. Not Odin's but your death must dare
foretell the great gods' dreaded, long awaited doom. My spell
grows weak. Go. Return to your hail. Fallow fields will soon bear
new seeds where Baldr bleeds in dreamtime sorrow, come the apocalypse."

(After Baldr's Dream)

Sigrdrifa to Sigurd

"Who ruins my sleep, who wakes me from a slumber
silent and pale as snow falling on woodlands?"
"Sigurd," he says, "Sigmund's son, fiercer
than his father, fresh from battle, from hands
and legs strewn on fields black as ravens."
"I have been sleeping," she says, "far longer
than men have suffered from sorrows." And he:
"I sing praise to the sun, the mighty fertile earth,
to what the sons of day must do to win victory,
and to goddesses who can foretell what men are worth."

"You must learn the mysteries of sea's journeys,"
 she says, "must cut into prow and rudder the secrets
of runes, burn them into oars so that no waves
break over your ships and drown you in regrets
for the sorrows that will befall you, listen to
what trees whispers, what cold winds tell you
of healing, how to weave new lives out of old,
find in bears' paws, wolves' claws, eagles' beaks
the answers to what the truly brave man seeks
as he drinks from the mead cup: what fate it's foretold."

"I know I am doomed," he says, "but I am no coward.
Nothing you say can frighten me." And she:
"Be blameless and honest to kin, but hard
as your father. Accept revenge, but seek it slowly
in honor of the dead. Keep your oaths truly
and close. A dreadful fate awaits all who break
them. Do not argue with fools, but, as due, take
time to speak truly. Avoid evil hags who blindly sit
by roads to deaden men's spirits, they are all filthy.
Never kiss a silver-bedecked beauty however tempted to do it.

And, lastly, guard against evil. Bury corpses deep
into the ground, whether dead from disease
or drowning or battle. They will not sleep
if not bathed, washed in warm water to ease
their descent into the grim pit, denied oblivion,
cast into Hel's chambers where memories rage
at men who grieve for their lies, loss of honor
long after their lives are over. If you could, die from old age,
the gods' greatest gift to men. But you can't. Now let me
rest forever. Fate is silent. No man speaks wisely. No god acts freely."

(After the Lay of Sigrdrifa)

Sigurd's Death

Oath-taker but not keeper-.
falsifier, deceiver,
Sigurd, a betrayed Brunhild seeks
your death. All those
she hates she wreaks
havoc upon, you, too close
to Gudrun, too far
from her, unwilling to pleasure
her. War after war
you've fought. What manly cure
for her desires did you
offer her, what wolf-meat,
what taste of snake you were too
quick to feast Guthorm on, what bees'
honeyed sweet?

While a raven calls to you from a tree,
Atli reddens his sword
in your blood to satisfy
his lust. Hear the word
of pine and oak, what's spoken
by stones as Hogni hacks
you to pieces and an unridden
black horse that lacks
only its rider
flies through the sky
like a Valkyrie
bearing no body
as night gets drunk on the moon
in its inhuman lamentation.

For the hour of woeful women's weeping
has begun, the hall chilly,
embers cold, their men riding,
fast as hawks from tree
to prey, through forests like prisoners
bereft of their chains,
foemen of Sigurd's kin, strangers
to peace, through high plains,
low valleys forever racing,
doomed destroyers
while the hero lies on a pyre—
his sword, his wound-wand, braided
with gold —waiting for the consuming fire,
ever unknown to him the rest of a plowman,
content, asleep on his bed.

(After the Codex Regius)

Riddles

To the Memory of Karen Nyboe Høghnissen and Eva-Marie Olga Høghnissen Weltner,
     Her Daughter, My Mother

1.

Early moonlight glares ice-white off Coney Island
as Karen shivers in the tide, a wet, heavy swim-
suit sagging off her body. Staring, her husband
smokes his clay pipe, his wavy silver hair thin
as a boy's, though he's years older than his young
wife. Snow geese beat their wings in a gray
sky, each flapping motion beautiful and strong.
København and Holstebro are a long, hard way
from Manhattan. Years after their only child is born,
a daughter, both of Henry's legs are amputated
against diabetes. Karen takes a lover, a Norwegian
sea-captain. Her husband understands, ill, worn-
out, a burden. After three years, the stalwart man
Karen adores returns to northern seas, never again to be happy.

So Karen and her daughter, soon after Eva's married,
book passage on a cargo-laden freighter bound for
Costa Rica. The waters their eyes follow as if led
by stars look sun-burnt, stranger than the mythic lore
Danes tell of the Northern lights in winter. Back home,
at night, Karen climbs to the roof to watch ships
sail from port to Europe. At parties, she wears becoming
tight blue or black dresses over her firm, girdleless
body. She never wears powder or lipstick on her lips,
and of her dark auburn hair she brags there isn't one gray
strand. When she dreams, she dreams of the gulf stream
sometimes, how it keeps her warm when swimming on a day
otherwise too icy cold to immerse herself in, stripped, naked,
her ruddy face taut with the force of her lover's last grim happiness.

2.

A brisk breeze blows from river to river, billowing
skirts, mussing hair, sending people scurrying
for their flying hats. The park is filled with children
playing, men and women relaxing, lallygagging,
lazying on a day when the air has just begun
to chill, summer waning. Ducks paddle on
the lagoon, kids toss balls, lovers lie side by
side on beach blankets.   My mother is swelling
more as I grow. She sits on a thick flat mossy
boulder observing the world, folks aimlessly,
gayly strolling through the park, ambling past
her, gliding like angels, she thinks, through the city's
happiest place. The world's at war, nothing lasts.
Why? Couples walk arm in arm. A skinny old man whispers
to rustling leaves. Clouds glide by serenely, promising showers.

Inside a thicket of bushes, a whistle blows. Laughter
follows. Another whistle is blown from behind
a tree. Antiphonal, dissonant music. A dog races
after a squirrel. What does she want to find
for her life that she's not yet found? Breezes
blow harder, die down, return. She dreads cold,
autumn's arrival. She wants time to stop, cease,
that dog, these kids, those lovers, that mad old
man, the birds flying freely through sighing trees,
the clouds, the wind, the sky; she wants it all to become
silently still, eternal. paradisal, erasing her fears
that nothing can stay as it is, unchanging, however dear
to her since even the child in her womb will be born to die
some day in this sad beautiful cruel world that's humanity's only home.

Flushed, she shudders, stands up, and brushes
dry leaves off her skirt. It's a long trip back
to Plainfield by subway and train. The weather's
changing quickly. Walking, heading south
on Fifth Avenue by the wall, she chances
on a few, lovely, cast aside curiosities that lack
only imagination to love them, stuffs some into
a pocket, relics she'll keep to show life's truth
to her children, how it sometimes shines: a blue
swatch of a silk scarf, a red bow caught between
bench slats, a swift's pinfeather, copper green,
tarnished pennies, crushed foil from a stick of chewing
gum hidden in crabgrass by a curb near the Plaza, valuing
each as if it satisfied her need to save all life's poor discarded things.

3.

Grandmother, Mother, if I were to forget you
I'd lead a hapless life. I've given
you my sorrows without meaning to,
leaving you again, like men like me back then

had to. No family survives without
its common sorrows. Freedom is never
innocent, is it?, always also about
loss to someone. In an Ozu film I remember,

an aging mother says, "Life is disappointing."
She was talking mainly about her children,
but also her lost dreams, her suffering,
her wifely loneliness, how love never begins again.

Long ago, I watched a spotted, dun-colored
bird, a fledging, hesitantly flying from
its nest in a tall oak, forced
to leave by instinct, abandoning its home.

It soared high, borne by breezes through trees,
young and free, though still diminutive,
until it perched, blinking, chirping on an eave,
of our house, as if to declare, "I'm here, alive."

Not so much a lesson, a fable, this story,
as a riddle without an answer: why be born
at all, and, if you are alive already,
why suffer to wait for another dawn?

4.

Say, unborn, I dream of a good man, a visitor
to my world. Nothing must harm him, not hunger
or thirst, not illness or old age. It is he who
will accompany me, in years to come through

time, not on a mission, but someone who will serve
other's trust faithfully, safe in our homeland, safe far
from it, free from bitterness, never to swerve
cowardly from perilous ways. I'll never bar

him from our bed, will be even more than a lover,
one never a burden to the other. Once I depart
my kin's company, look, swings by his thigh,
below the belt, within the folds of his clothes,

a thing most magical. If this is truly, really who I
am to be, before I'm born, tell me what he knows
of me. Solve this riddle for me, dearest Mormor,
Mother, whisper his name, you who are my progenitors,

who will free me from the unseen dark, love me; bringing
me forth, understand me, speak to me of everything
I'll become as if life were to be not only a puzzle but a wonder
as he and I wander through it, loving each other, enduring what we suffer.

5.

Womb of the wold that bore me cold,
dark to the world, unknown to woe,
dark to the mind, mysterious thing,
a living soul, out of nothing, I came
crying. If I can, I'll stand wayside, tall,
gleaming, climbing timbered cliffs,
speechless though I am, helpless as a new-
born lamb or calf. Near the tides
I'll build our dwelling, riddle-riddled
where all's conundrum, all that's said
spoken in whispers, in rainy weather
weeping by the fire: gladden me there,
beloved, for what grieves me sorely,
the hunger, longing for water I confessed
to you early. Hold me tightly. Name me.

V

Verdancy

Green, I love you, too, green. Grass's mute green,
a green to lie under, moss-dark, democratic,
Whitman's fall-fateful leaves in the unseen
viridescence of death, the earth's verdant music
heard in forest's sibilance, across wind's breathing,
the pulse of green things rising, the green
of ancient rivers swelling, streams newborn,
the icy green of winter as it turns to nothing
but a scene for mourners. What can it mean,
the green of your eyes as you were torn
from my arms, from my sight in the green
days of our passions, summer fields, meadows
in shadows, the lush growth of leafy sorrows,
you without me flowing toward the emerald infinity
of your desires, the Darro converging with the Genil
below, cloudy green will o wisp misty olive-bearing sea-
bound rivers bearing the flow of our post-orgasmic bodies
suddenly quieted and still.

(After Lorca)

The Battle of Megara

An unvisited well and a white cypress grove stand
near a nameless stone, less lonely than it is. Go
to the spring circling its trees, to the seaside land
near the fields of the fallen. You may know
it from history books. Wash your hands in its cold,
cleansing water. No young soldiers still guard
this earth, now part of history. A child of the old
gods and the unplowed earth left unscarred
by armies, he belongs forever to the open sky.
For Plato, the beloved, the soul's journey's desirous
of quenching its thirst in waters that never run dry.
But the war arose and destroyed him first. It is impious
to forget, we're warned. Yet he lies beneath our feet at rest
and forgotten. Perhaps his name was Achelous, like the twice-blessed
river. But that is only a wild guess about a grave so noble and so antonymous.

Nocturnal Moths

A November-deep cold grips the air as darkening
clouds hover over oaks, maple, spruces, long-
leaf and pitch pines. A woodchuck's festering
pelt lies entangled in kudzu. Something's wrong
with his soul. At sunset, the sky smolders
with a chill clarity as if heaven had suddenly
turned translucent, like ice melting on a fiery
earth. It's time to lock doors, latch the shutters.
If it happens now, it'll never occur again, says
the Book of Ages. The man's face is white
as grubs, his tired body lying half-lit where in spring
he grows asters and tulip roses. The sun's dying rays
slip out of the sky. A tiger and a lunar moth fly bright
with moonlight by him, more alive than he is to life's mute wonder.

(After Ozu)

Sun Music

1.

Rust-speckled apples, wild roses dangle
from trees and bushes over a lake
mallards drift on. One boy floats
beside another in the calm, sun-
warmed water. The day in its quiet
beauty seems to belong to dawn
forever, like an old boat cradled
by lapping waves tied to its dock.

When winter arrives, autumn's already
stripped the trees. Where there was
sunlight, now there's blue ice,
dusky shadows covering snow.
Harsh winds pressing against
them, fences creak, gates rattle.
The days grow cold and sunless,
light more hesitant, hovering over the horizon.

Do children come too late to understanding?
To slumber and evening and distress
instead? Grown old, always dreaming
of a world that was theirs? As if trying
to gather flowers, dark and cold
in the gloom and shade of the sun's
far side of the forest, in the midst
of a winter slumber that cannot comfort them?

2.

Grant the old one more spring, summer,
another autumn. Let words, thoughts
ripen their lives before they leave. Let
them come to fruition, like birds
singing deep in woods at twilight,
their songs too sadly beautiful to be heard.

For music alone endures beyond silence
as if the dead could hear it,
however confused they are
by it, by being dead, unable
to remember what it once meant
to mourn for others more than themselves.

Yet does it not remain true? How like
a rite Bach's, Mozart's, Schubert's
music is, suspended between
night and day in that borderland
before dawn where people once
gathered to pray, waiting for sun to return.

    (After Hölderlin)

The Godly Earth

1.

Hölderlin said the dead might find contentment
in their deaths, walking at last with gods
always beside them. Amidst its flickering
shadows, they'd realize no lasting tranquility,

only an eternal quietude, like Eurydice's
after the last Orphic note had sounded
from her lover's lyre, his heavenly music
unable to revive her twice. And that is

the saddest intimation of it: even tragic
music belongs to the sun, like bread
and wine nourishing life with their holy
intoxications, joyful, if sober celebrations

that make us stay awake at night sometimes,
we, too, waiting for the sun to rise
for our eyes, our souls, to be revived by
its light, only to find it's Phaeton diving into the sea.

2.

Long after winter's images are fulfilled, though
invisible, its cold has lasted so long it weighs
heavily on us, the fields emptied of snow,
and the views clearer, it's true, but winter stays
forever in us, the storms, the rain, the cloudy, sunless days.

Yet, as restful as a holiday feels, so is the relief of year's end.
What are seasons if not questions waiting for
answers? Spring arrives, wild flowers send
up their shoots, new leaves appear before our eyes
and the sun sings unto our godly earth again with all its splendor.

(After Scardanelli)

The Deposition

In Caravaggio's version, the bleak dark background
of the deposition is painted blacker than tar
or coal, like a nightmare in which nothing's found
except suffering, pain, more death, Mary
wailing, the beloved disciple bending far
over the body, his cloak red as if blood-
soaked, stunned Nicodemus staring out to see
who else might be looking, women who'd stood
by the cross mourning, imploring. His body
is being laid not in a grave or tomb but on a hefty
slab of thick stone. But where is the somber light
cast on the scene coming from, too late for the sun?
John's hand covers the wound in Jesus' side in adoration.
Or is it love, that compassionate sorrow funereal in its radiant rites?

Corpus Christi in Venice

It's like perfumes of intense red flowers, like incense
from a pyre. The campanile's bell towers
shadow children playing by the basilica. Silence.
No tides lapping on the palazzo. Two rowers
sleeping in a gondola. The late afternoon sun
is scalding, white, blanching the canals. A priest
with a Buddha smile strolls past. The light is waxen,
like melting air. It is the day of the feast,
white and purple banners everywhere in honor
of His body. Enter its burning light to make
your penance. The eye is an endless embarkation
painting chalky brushstrokes along the horizon
between a silvery sea and feathery clouds. For
what is vision if untransformed into art? You, who take
me there, tell me, what offering, what obeisance
suffices to commune with it, the sun past its zenith,
the flowers and wreaths hung from windows and doors,
a flock of red-throated loons over head and a mammoth
fountain past which, far off, you can almost see the cypress
trees of San Michele, as if lightly brushed in, delicate as a lover's caress?

Preparing for Bed

A light feathery orange, bold downy red
cardinal sings to a boy on a schoolyard
swing while his sister rocks on a teeter-
totter. Soon, it will be time for bed.
The bird blinks at both with sad regard.
Where are their father, their mother?
They've been left on their own to play
since the park was said to be safe. But they
have been deceived. A darkened doorsill
alone awaits their belated return. Do not say
they have not been warned. A waxbill
finch in another tree warbled of the chill
in the air, the coming northerly cold when
children lie awake at night, dreamless and forgotten.

VI

North County Country

Walk ahead of me. I'll follow you.
I know where you're going:
into the north coast's old-
growth forest, the earth
damp from last night's
showers, leaves, needles,
branches, twigs, ferns
dripping as if from dew.
A thrush flutters off
its perch, twittering, its song,
flute-like, piercing,
awakening the wilderness,
and the nearby seas as they
crash against crumbing cliffs.

Wine-dark ivy twines round
boughs and thickly barked
trees, spruces and redwoods
whose spectral, almost
human shadows you hike
beside as late dawn seeps
through the canopy,
its light, pale yellow,
pastel orange, blossoming
like mountain lilies peeking
through bushes, shimmering
like a sun-lit creek flowing
more rapidly, wandering,
more nomadic as it nears the Pacific.

Even at midday, the forest
is tenebrous, immemorial,
the air dusky and chill,
heavy with the musty
fragrance of decaying
humus and wet, earthy
moss. The shallow stream
you seek gleams like
ivory in the half-light
as it lets you follow it
as far as those who love
life can go, past their
shadows into the night-darkened
valley below treeless hills and cliff face.

Its is the precipitous grief
you fear of dying alone.
A headwind is battering
the forest, beating it
down, fires consume
it, nations are failing,
the sun is fading,
and the north will soon
be betrayed by night.
Call it old age, the rage
you'd hurl against it,
the way the world is who
you are, the rain, the flames,
and the wilderness vanishing before you.

Poetry and Silence

Friend, if I might still call you my friend,
destroy my work or forget it,
do what you will with it, end
it at last. It's over anyway. Not a bit
will survive the future, that vast sea
called uncertainty, though Poseidon is
known to be thirsty sometimes,
but for wine, not poems. I'll miss
it, of course, the play of rhymes,
the musical measures, the artsy formality.

Some seek to be driven into a frenzy
by it, like the god who hides in his
shrine at Pytho where Corybantes
strike their shrilly clanging cymbals;
beg songs to madden them, seize
their spirits, arouse the furies
within them with their sirens' calls
to ecstasy and rage, a passionate
poetry, freely if wily polemical,
like a song to liberate the disconsolate.

Human rage is the only weapon no Doric
sword can conquer nor Jupiter crack
with thunder. Prometheus made us
out of every creature there is in nature:
the lion attacking its prey, Atreus
forcing Thyestes to devour, like an epicure,
his children, the cruelties of soldiers
pillaging, savaging people and their cities.
How much of poetry is inspired by its writers'
demanding you yield like them to their inner furies?

Wrath, pride, despair equally confuse us
into saying, aloud or on paper, what
should be left, kept quiet. To refuse
to speak or write more words that
make others suffer; to erase all
you've done, written, its every letter
as if compelled to follow the call
of poetry, of art; to leave instead unsaid
what you'd meant to say: is this not what dead
poets should tell us? How peaceful silence is, how bitter.

(After Horace 1.16)

Clear Cut

I write these few parched words out
of a dried well of sorrow, an empty
wine cup of grief. I was a man
of the wood kind, sapling to stout
oak, yet stalwart shipboard, at sea
never wayward, no task called to I ran
from. My people were forest-proud.
pledged words truly, glad we did so.
Where I now lie, I hear not a sound,
no cry of robin, no spring song of cuckoo.

In rainy weather, by a lingering hearth,
my wife weeps for my wanderings,
the cold in the heart of my heart,
thatch frost-crusted as she sings
of life's bitterness, sea's breakers
crashing, rein-less horses at water's
edge racing over shell shards and sand,
hoard and horses, torch and brand,
the nightly raids for more gold and gold-
braided locks, women raped, stolen, then sold.

Our lips, hers and mine, swore nothing
would divide us, not even dying,
me a marked man, mourning-browed,
who found above coverts—where thorns,
nettles thrived and the black banked
hollows of caves gaped wide to warn
me of exile—the dark knotted knoll,
the pine stand twisted by fierce winds
where I would fall, another old oak bole
up-rooted, the forest family, my birthright kin.

It is always dry weather as wives weep by
hearths now. And I today? Who am I
if not clear-cut, what greed's
made and given us once the old
wild places gone, what the living need
from it undone, forever unsaid
like a story you were never told
of how the green world was made
for its own sake, yet bought and sold until
men gnaw on bones like wolves, red-eyed and deathly still.

A Wanderer in Saga Land

to the Memory of the Medievalist Dan Calder (1942-1984)

Waves taut as the haunches of horses, whip-
like manes, groundswell and surge, tidal barrage
of an island's beaches, its harbor leeward, ship-
safe when stormy. Wind-swept cliffs, the courage
it takes to live there, stark with icy desolations.
Why stay? The way of homebound men is to be
terns at sea, flying over unknown oceans,
ravenous, hunting in deep waters, cold, salty,
islands past blinding horizons. His boat is ready
to sail, glowing at sunrise like a ship set on fire,
the dead and their hoard in it burning at dawn,
gifted with gold, oar-steered and steady as his desire
to sail elsewhere, insatiably hungry, his spirit re-born
to go where maps fall silent and all eyes see more keenly.

A nameless farer, loss-burdened, unarmed, unshielded,
laden with sorrows, fears, crossing streams deepened
by spring floods, slick black crows flying overhead,
a hope-thwarted seeker of keel-sure seas, slogging
through mud, lost in woods, fed by hunger, dead
to the earth, heart-sick at bloodshed, sinking
into doldrums, mountains darker than the darkest
nights, unlocking pain's word-hoard, the ways
of wilderness, fighting in mead halls as a test
of strength between him and the gods who raise
his enemies out of their spilled seed, hearth ashes
whistling, whining in the wind, his breast swelling,
doomed to be ever journeying, ever sailing, passing
through life fate-forked, a cascading rock, an oak as it crashes.

The Death of King Arthur

In the neighborhood where Bryan Waddell lived and died, the old
gables seem to have been stuck arbitrarily on sharply pitched roofs.
There is little landscaping around the houses anymore, only an occa-
sional bush or shrub planted in sandy soil and left to die. There are
no more gardens. A few old cars are parked in driveways that are
overgrown with patches of high grass and weeds. What's left of lawns
is mostly ignored, littered with car parts, twists of machinery, flower
pot shards, or crumpled cardboard boxes scattered over them. Roof
trusses sag.

I'm glad I escaped from it in time, what was my home too once,
long ago, now lost.

It was in that down-on-your-luck part of eastern Camlann Coun-
ty that Bryan spent his final years, born there when it was a happier
place. His wood house badly needed paint and repair. A few sheets of
tar paper and sand imitations of brick had peeled away and lay where
they'd fallen, who knows when. His side porch sat on cinder blocks,
the tin roof over it had rusted. It had not been always like that. It
had not always been a small town waste land.

The remains of Camlann County's old growth woods and the near-
ly primeval wilderness hidden deep within its borders used to reach to
Bryan's backyard and those of his neighbors, reminders of the ex-
pansive, free, and green world into which we all had been born many
decades ago.

Now it seems to be mostly a world of scattered, cast off things, a
world of feverish, bright colors that have swiftly faded, whose people
seem to have succumbed to the hard-won lesson that finally nothing is
worth the human effort and suffering it takes to try to keep it safe and
good for the future, to hold onto at least some remnants of the past
when everything around it seems intent on destroying it. Maybe there
is too little left to remind us of what any place, anyone was really like
after they've died. But in Camlann folks have given up the ancient
struggles they've tired of.

Ben Caudle had been a presence in my youth mostly by accident
and only in a minor way, not all that important in the greater scheme
of things, if there is one. Ben was still young, just a little over twenty,
when he inherited the Texaco Station after his father had died early of

lung cancer and his mother and sisters had moved to Lumberton with her new husband whom she'd married, the gossips clucked, too quickly, like the baby born shortly after.

I barely knew Ben but I hung around his station a lot when I was nine or ten with little else to do during the long summers. It was an easy hike to the station from my home along a curvy, quiet country road that snaked along the southern parts of the county's then still pristine wilderness.

I guess I was lonely and longing for company. Ben never asked me what I was doing there or what I wanted. I was just a little kid. He left me alone to goof about and listen all I liked. So did Bryan, his good buddy. They made me feel welcome, like a little cousin.

I wanted to thank Bryan for what he and Ben have given me when I was a kid before it was too late, how they more than tolerated me those summers, how easily they put up with my moodiness back then. We were all getting seriously old, after all. And Ben had just died. I wanted to learn what I could about his life, about the parts of it I never saw when I was young or never learned about later. So I called Bryan who surprisingly remembered me, the little smart aleck kid who was always wandering around, eyes wide open, and laughed at his jokes.

"I was Ben Caudle's best friend," Bryan Waddell bragged right away shortly after I'd arrived at his house, a few days after Ben's death, handing me a can of beer. I told him I was back home for a week or two and that I'd been living up north for fifty years and had returned to visit only a handful of times before. My parents died in late middle age. Everyone else I'd once known there had moved away or died, too. One friend from my childhood, my age, who lives in Denver now, but has a sister still living in the county, called me to let me know Ben had died, I said. He thought I'd want to know.

I'd rented a car and drove down without stopping along the way and was staying in a motel off Route 401, wondering once I was here why I'd returned at all. My childhood was hardly a happy one. Whose is really? But I liked Ben. His was a curious soul.

I was too late for the funeral. That's why I'd sought out Bryan and asked him about Ben.

But after I'd told him all I needed to, Bryan just stared at me, furrowing his brow before he said anything. He'd looked distracted or annoyed or maybe just puzzled.

After a strained few minutes, he nodded and said, "I've just been

wondering if I should ever have called myself Ben's 'best friend,' be-
cause I wasn't. Charlie Whitaker was Ben's best friend back in those
early days. But that was all so long ago, who knows or cares any-
more about who was best and who was second best? Would Ben? Of
course not. Good, better, best. All a lot of nonsense, isn't it? About
everything?

"We three started palling around while we were still young boys,
barely out of diapers, wandering the countryside and woods alone to-
gether during the long summer of the worst year of the epidemic that
hit Camlann County particularly hard in nineteen forty eight. You're
too young to remember that, that plague, those locusts on the land,
devouring the bodies of children, how awful it was."

"Not so young," I said. "I remember it, too, in a way from what
my brothers told me."

"Even so," he said and sighed before taking another drag on his
cigarette, letting the smoke fill the room before talking some more.

"A lot of kids had died that summer or been paralyzed. Kids we
knew. It was terrifying. Like the protective hand of the Lord had
been withdrawn from us. Everyone was scared. That's when the
quarantining began. After the first deaths. Schools closed. No public
gatherings. Swimming pools drained. The only movie theater locked
for the duration. Some folks even stopped going to church on Sundays
and Wednesday nights.

"Me and Ben had just turned ten. Charlie was a year younger. We
were inseparable," Bryan said. "We would have been anyway prob-
ably since our families' tobacco fields bordered each other in those
days, before farmers started selling off the land, and we were all good,
God-fearing Baptists, too, though the Caudles and my folks attended
True Life Cornerstone and the Whitakers Mt. Tabor Full Gospel.

"I don't know. Maybe the threat of the polio brought us closer than
we might have been otherwise. It's hard to say all these years later.
You know how it used to be with kids. Friends were friends for life.
No one needed to say that then. It was just how it was.

"But it's also true that we knew if we just stuck together we'd be
safe. That we wouldn't get sick and die or, God forbid, get paralyzed
for life. That scared us worse than the dying. To be stuck in an iron
lung forever. What God would allow that? I still can't answer that. I
wish I could. Can you?"

My family hadn't known the Waddells or the Watkins or Caudles, except by sight. It was a small county. But we were Presbyterians, and my father owned a hardware store. It was a matter of caste, sometimes strictly observed, sometimes not at all. Much of it depended on how old you were and how long your people had dwelled in Camlann County. It took a century or more for roots to dig deep enough to say you belonged there.

But I saw Bryan and Ben and Charlie at the station all the time those summers I went wandering on my own. Like Ben, Bryan was ten years older than me and an impressive guy, a football star and all that, and had made a name for himself later, still young, as a hotshot, go-to insurance salesman to the county's farmers and small store owners. He was popular, fated for success. His business flourished.

It was obvious to everyone that he and Ben would be lifelong good buddies. Given the difference in the way they ended up living their lives, their friendship became famous, then curious. Somehow it thrived for more than six decades through all the twists of fate during which Ben had always lived alone in the cramped one room apartment he'd built for himself above his station, surviving mostly on RC Colas and peanut butter or egg sandwiches and endless hard work. That's what Bryan said, admiring him for what he called his forbearance and patience, yet confused by his need for solitude.

Everyone in Camlann was aware of Ben's strange, reclusive ways. That was never news. It was just how he was. They tolerated, even accepted it because he was known as a good, decent man, a fine mechanic who ran an honest business. Most people in the county filled their cars or trucks up at Ben's Texaco. It was just the thing to do, almost like going to church. No one minded, or much minded, his eccentricities. He was a free-spirited soul, they'd say.

Especially when I was ten or maybe eleven, I liked hanging around there, listening to the men talk in their halting way when they were not staring out at the fields or up and down the highway or up at the sky, trying to see something faraway or think of something else to say. They were a reticent people, the men of Camlann County.

Yet, despite their long silences, they all clearly liked each other, got along, since they already knew each other so well any words would pretty much prove worthless anyhow. If they suffered from this or that, so what? That was the way of the world. I guess, as a kid, I admired them, their quiet, diffident ways without understanding any of the rest of it. Their pain, I mean. Their need for love. Their habitual unacknowledged loneliness, married or not, Ben's solitude most of all. I felt it accumulating in myself, even that young, gathering up my world's way of suffering inside me without my knowing it, just by watching it happen to others.

Once I had my license, I always bought my gas from Ben, too, as everybody else always did. If my car had problems, Ben or one of his mechanics would fix it. He was beloved all right, by everyone, but a bit of a local character, too, the butt of jokes I hope he never heard, that made me mad at the ease with which friends laughed at him.

He almost never dressed in anything except his bib overalls and denim shirts except on Sundays when he'd be seen sitting in a back pew alone wearing clean, freshly pressed jeans and a white shirt with a black string tie. That was his Sunday best, Sunday after Sunday.

Overalls wore well, he'd say if asked, and bore hard scrubbing and laundering well, too, and didn't fray fast. It just made sense. It was practical, he'd say. He was that rare sort of man who showed no trace of vanity. But he could be stubborn.

What was the oddest fact about Ben Caudle, odder, that is, than his insistence on being left alone most of the time or his refusal of every invitation to supper he ever received, the truly inexplicable fact about him, everyone agreed, was his passion for a Viennese tenor by the name of Richard Tauber who sang a kind of music no one else in Camlann County enjoyed or had ever even heard of, songs from Austrian or German operettas and arias by Mozart and the like and some Schubert lieder.

Ben could never get enough of that man's singing, day or night playing his Richard Tauber LPs. He had to order the records from a store in New York City. It was a mystery how he had first heard him. On the radio maybe? Ben was a mysterious man, you could hear folks say, whispering about him from time to time. Meaning, I knew, not like them. And so lonely. Loneliness, though common as rats, felt like a sin in Camlann County in those days. It probably still does, one of those sins everyone has to forgive others for because they've known it too often in themselves not to.

I asked him once, "Why Tauber?"

He set his pliers aside on a jack and looked thoughtful, surprising me by taking my question seriously. "I don't know," he said. "He's seen a lot. Felt a lot. You can hear it in his voice. Some happier world maybe, but full of sadness. Nostalgia."

I thought to myself, Nostalgia. What a strange word for Ben Caudle to use. It did not fit the picture. I was a snotty little kid sometimes. Maybe I still am.

But Ben was mysterious in other ways, too. That was why Bryan Waddell so gladly welcomed me into his home, I guess. He wanted to talk to me about what he had seen, it was like a vision he'd had, he said, right after Ben had died.

I suspect he felt free to tell me about it, and maybe only me, because I had left Camlann County for worlds elsewhere long ago. I was now at best a casual visitor, an outsider, a tourist. I would be leaving to go back to Providence soon. I was someone it was safe for him to tell his story to. And he knew I was a writer. Right off, he insisted that he wanted me to write his story down and have it published somewhere and so make it real that way, as if print, written words, could immortalize the truth of what he was bearing witness to.

What he'd seen might prove to be nonsense, or crazy, but it was what he believed. And he wanted what he'd seen to be believed by others, including me, the outside witness, the bearer and conveyer of that truth as he saw it. Which is what all serious writing ought to be about, isn't it? To bear witness to the evidence of a vision otherwise unseen?

Since the two of them, he and Ben, were the same age, Bryan sensed his death would soon follow his friend's. "It's best that way," he said. "more real and necessary."

He was getting ready to die. "Look at me, he said, "crippled with arthritis, gray and stinky as an old skunk, no use to anyone after my missus died ten years ago and the kids moved away."

It, that imminent departure, made what he was about to tell me that more urgent. I could hear it in his voice, that fear of vanishing altogether.

"When we were twelve, me and Ben and Charlie went camping together out by Rawlings Lake almost every weekend. You must remember where that was," Bryan said, "way the hell out by the Chatanooka Cut where the old Indians had farmed. It's been what they call developed long since, though the lake's still there, part of a park now. I never have understood it. Maybe young folks enjoy it the way it is now, like a big cement swimming pool. I don't know. It feels wrong to me. But I don't belong here anymore.

"Anyway, Charlie could sleep no matter where or how we bunked, but Ben was always restless when he was away from home, getting up in the middle of the night every night and not just to pee either. He might stay out till daybreak, wandering.

"So, curious as I was even then about his ways, I followed him once when he left our pup tent and watched him from a sufficient distance for him not to see me as he waited out the night by the lake, the eastern sky already burning red over the horizon as waves gently lapped the shore, a white mist steaming off the lake. It was going to be a beautiful morning.

"I kind of tiptoed over and asked him what he was doing. He blushed and then said, straight out, he was waiting for the ghosts of the county's long ago lost Indians to reappear, paddling their canoes, trying with their wide nets to catch the light as the end-of-night-setting moon shone on the water mingled with the fiery red of dawn. That's almost exactly what he said. In those words.

"An odd string of words to remember, I know. But I do. Ben was a strange person even then. Poetic, yet still just a kid. He wanted to see them. He wanted to see if those olden time people could really do it, if the legends were true, that they could really catch the dawn in nets meant for fishing bass and trout.

"You know he never married. No woman would put up with him, our elders would say. Maybe they were right, but I'm not so sure. He'd courted a few back in the day. Nothing ever came of it.

"But I do know he was heartbroken when Charlie was killed at Khe Sahn. We all were. Afterward Ben just let himself go, gave up, I guess, at thirty. He just became old and then seriously older faster than most of us and yet, except for me, pretty much outlasted those we'd grown up with anyway. Isn't that strange? God's plans for us and all? The best way to live is not to try to make sense of it, I reckon.

"When he heard the news, Ben broke down and cried. And he let me see him like that. The only time. I never told a soul. He was devastated.

"Late in his life, his eyes became sun-hardened, and his hands and arms, already gnarled from working in tobacco fields when he was young and needed cash, were often torn by rose bush thorns which he seemed to be forever pruning. Obsessively, you know?

"During his last few years, he had to use sticks to walk with, jagged poles he'd cut from a blighted oak and then carved to look like two snakes stretched out to full length, embracing. Beautiful objects, really, like works of art.

"When I first saw those sticks, I recalled how he'd almost wept when, years before, he found two big old kings flattened by a semi on the road in front of his Texaco, lying there like shiny black crepe paper strips twisted in a double S. He peeled them off the asphalt and hung them up in the lavatory until Carter Young complained about

100

how they looked demonic and would put a curse on the station if not the whole county.

"That was about the time Ben started seeing or hearing signs in things, too, maintaining they were hinting at the world's future, like omens given us in the shapes of clouds or trees' shadows, the uncanny heart shape of a rock he picked up in a corn field, the songs of swallows or orioles, the roar of thunder, the fiery sparkle in a cat's eye, the thickness of a man's calluses or the lines in his palms, omens that had proven true sometimes, he swore.

"The last day I saw him alive he was sitting in the shade of a giant mimosa, wearing his pork-pie hat and a denim jacket even though it was August, eating one of the plastic packaged white bread pimento cheese sandwiches he sold at the station and drinking an RC from its cooler. He even finished a whole can of Vienna sausages, licking his fingers after, then shivered, complaining of a chill, though it was hot as hell even in the shade. When he stood up, his trousers drooped over the mud-spattered brogans he got for free five years before when Layton Brigham passed on to glory and left his clothes for Ben to wear. New clothes, to Ben's way of thinking, he'd worn proudly, too, grateful to Layton.

"It was getting late. Or so Ben said, though it was barely seven thirty. Sort of half crawling or sliding, he dragged himself upstairs to his room and put on one of his Tauber records. They all sounded the same to me and all were in German, a language that in this county nobody understood or wanted to.

"Tauber was Jewish, Ben had explained to me, so it was all right. He meant to excuse only the German part of it, of course. The rest needed no excuse or explanation on his part. Camlann County had lost seven of its sons to the fight against those people, seven good and decent guys. Hank Williams and Roy Acuff were good enough for me. But for Ben the only singing voice worth listening to was Tauber's. I still can't understand it. Do you?

"The disc was badly worn, crackling like a spitting fire. I walked upstairs and peeked in. He was resting on his always unmade bed, his arms wrapped round the record jacket. Four or so hours later, he died, right around midnight, the coroner guessed.

"One of his long time mechanics found him early the next morning. He and I officially identified the body for the sheriff, though of course there was no doubt about it. Everybody knew Ben by sight. The LP jacket he was holding onto said it was The Land of Smiles he'd been listening to. I don't much care for irony myself, if that's what it was."

Bryan suddenly stopped talking, stood up, wandered around his dank, cramped, musty living room, stared out the window for a while as the light inside drifted toward evening, lit another Camel, and sat back down, sighing.

"Now this is where my story becomes stranger," Bryan warned me, frowning some. "You knew it had to."

"Maybe I'd caught it from Ben," he said "I mean the way woods called to me, too, some nights now I've become antique, when I cannot sleep. The night he died, I found myself like a sleepwalker walking deep into the forest, as if it had never changed, as if the woods and Rawlings Lake and all the rest of that world we'd spent so much time in when we were young, had returned to its old self somehow. Later, I had no memory about how I had gotten there. But I wasn't merely dreaming. I swear to you I wasn't.

"I was wide awake. But I had stepped back into the past. It all looked familiar, of course, yet I felt lost in it too, in those woods, until I saw Ben walking toward what we'd called our lake, not the Rawlings', but his and mine and Charlie's. It was ours. It belonged to us. So we renamed it: Bry-Ben-Char Lake. Sounds almost Indian, don't it?

"Ben was hiking fine and upright through the pine and oak and spruce forest without needing his sticks, unbothered, unimpeded by the thickets of brush and ivy that used to slow us down, resisting our boyish eagerness to reach the water to strip and swim in it, the lake that he was heading steadily toward one last time, not looking back, free and easy as a kid. When he reached its banks, he stopped, stood on a flat rock, and waited. Just waited."

Bryan paused, as if tired, stopped talking for maybe five or six minutes. His living room was fully dark now. I could barely make out his face. His silence worried me. Should I leave without hearing the rest? Let him sleep?

I offered to get him a glass of water. He shook bis head. I sat back down.

"During that summer of '48," he said, "Ben and I and Charlie had found on a few large ancient oak trees carvings we were sure had been made by the Indians who'd lived here long before our people claimed their land as ours. Carvings of faces so old and overgrown they could barely be seen peering through the bark, staring at us, as if almost pleading with us to be freed from that imprisonment.

"One, maybe the clearest surviving, had been carved on an enormous beech that was nearing the end of its days after having lived three or more centuries, it looked like. 'That's me when I grow old,' Ben said, 'resurrected in that tree.' And then, when Charlie gently touched it, explored the face, felt its features so tenderly, I guess I became sure of what I knew already.

"It's hard for me to tell anymore when that thought first occurred to me. You know what I mean. We were just boys, but there was a part of Ben and a part of Charlie that was theirs and theirs only, that belonged only to them, to each other, and never would be mine to share. It made me jealous.

"Envious, too. It was strange how strongly I felt that envy still, even the day after Ben had died. Because I knew he was dead already before I knew it factually, you see? I did not need to be told or look at his dead body. Why else was I there, in those woods? I must have been expected, been invited by something, some spirit.

"It was getting close to dawn when I heard someone paddling a canoe across the water to the western bank. Ben tuned toward where the sound was coming from expectantly, as if that was what he had been waiting for most of the night.

"And as it approached closer to the shore I saw it was Charlie, young as he'd been when he left for 'Nam, paddling the boat over the water toward Ben. It was him, really him, Charlie Watkins all right, no ghost, no apparition, I promise you. It was Charlie. And Ben, without any hesitation, waded into the water, and with Charlie's help lifted himself into the boat and sat down behind him while Charlie steadily, silently paddled him back across toward where the woods were densest, darkest, hard to see your way to where you were going even after dawn had illuminated it, even at noon, in the fullness of daylight. It was always night in there."

Bryan stopped talking again and gazed at me warily through the dark which now divided us to where I sat in an upholstered chair across from him in his smoky, slightly musty, unlit, moonless living room. "You don't believe me," he said, disappointed.

"Does it matter?" I said.

He sipped his beer, now long gone flat and warm. "Yes. A forest might tell you truths most people would prefer to ignore. That's why I am telling you this. You say you're a writer, so write it down. Promise me.

"Promise me you'll say I, Bryan Waddell, swear I believe Ben Caudle always knew where he was going, where he was headed, what he was destined for, just as he knew who would be paddling the old canoe that would carry him across to it. He already knew his life's whole story and, when it was almost over, I believe his spirit left his body, abandoned it on its bed in the room over his filling station so it could rise to meet Charlie. It's what let him die easy, with that funny smile on his face, that hope, that expectation.

"I can still see him, picture him, hoot owls bidding him safe journeys, as he let his fingers sift through the water, cool to the touch, soothing his pain, washing his long life away, as he listened to the water lap against the canoe, drip off the paddle, watching open-eyed and happy, by dawn, as the leaves and twigs drifted with the currents that, stronger than Charlie's long, wide, carved paddle, carried them both across, together again. They were being freed from life, released from its limits together. Don't you see?"

Did I? After Bryan died of an aneurysm only three days after he'd told me his story, I decided, before I drove back home, as a kind of memorial to him and Ben and Charlie, I'd explore Rawlings Lake by myself as I had done when I was a boy, too, roaming around it, hiking in the woods, the wilderness, as Ben and his two great friends used to at the same young age.

I started my trek at Ben's Texaco Station, closed until further notice. It took me over two and a half hours to reach the woods and the eastern shore of the lake.

Algae had started to infest some of the coves and inlets. I noticed an old pier, which had probably fallen years before, covered by weeds and succumbing to pond scum. New housing crowded the edges of what remained of the northern woods. The park close by it appeared to be little used. Maybe I visited it too early in the day. But it looked lonely and unwanted and desolate.

And yet, as I stood on the shore, unfazed by the passage of time, staring far off, I knew I was waiting, too, like Ben, like Bryan in pursuit of him, his spirit, longing to hear the lake lap against the hull of a canoe or even a rowboat maybe, being paddled or oared toward where they'd stood, where I stood, though I couldn't see him, the one I was anticipating, because of the mist and cloud-covered sunrise.

How long would I need to wait before he paddles his dugout or canoe near enough to the shore for me to wade into the water where he'd help me into the little boat that would carry us back across?

Or, if none of that had ever really happened, if that anticipation were nothing but a kind of half-mad fantasy or myth or fable, a hope shared only by deluded souls like us, at least I'd be able to say that I'd seen him at dawn one day, too, if only for a moment, if only in a dream Bryan had had like an uncertain, elusive memory, expressed through his story of it by which I'd heard, too clearly, vividly for it to have been only imaginary, the lake's gentle waters slapping against craggy rocks, rippling in the reeds as he greeted me; by which, listening to it, I'd felt his warm breath on my face again as he turned toward me and pointed across the waters to the distant shore where we were going, into that darkness, into that forest.

Not Charlie. Not Ben. Not even Bryan. But him. Me and him Our unfinished lives together, returning. Even now, from long ago. Leith.

Then sir Bedwere toke the kynge uppon has bak and so wente with hym to the watirs syde. And whan they were there evyn faste by the banke hoved a lytell barge with many fayre ladyes in hit, and amonge hem all was a quene, and all had blak hoodis. And all they wepte and shryked when they saw king Arthur.

"Now put me into that barge," seyde the kynge.

And so he died sofftely, and there receyved hym three ladyes with grete mournyng.

And so they sette hem downe, and in one of their lappis kynge Arthure layde hys hede.

And than the quene seyde,

"A, my dere brothir! Why have ye taryed so longe frome me. Alas, thys wounde on your hede hath caught overmuch coulde!"

And anone they rowed fromward the londe, and sir Bedyvere behylde all tho ladyes go frowarde hym. Then sir Bedwere cryed and seyde,

"A, my lorde Arthur, what shall becom of me, now ye go frome me and leve me here alone among myne enemyes?"

"Comforte theyself," seyde the kynge, "and do as well as thou mayst for in me ys no trust for to trust in. For I muste into the vale of Avylyon to hele me of my grevous wounde. And if thou here nevermore of me, pray for my soule!"

But ever the quene and ladyes wepte and shryked, that hit was pité to hyre. And as sone as sir Bedwere had loste the syght of the barge he wepte and wayled, and so toke the foreste and wente all that nyght.

Peter Nissen Weltner was raised in suburban New Jersey and piedmont North Carolina. He received his AB from Hamilton College where he majored in English with a minor in Philosophy, and his Ph.D. in English from Indiana University, where his inside major was Renaissance Poetry and Drama, his outside one in the School of Letters. His dissertation, Translated Mortality, was a close reading of the court plays of John Lyly. He taught for thirty-seven years in the English Department of San Francisco State, retiring in 2006.

His first published work, beginning in the seventies, appeared in English Literary Renaissance, Parnassus, Ironwood, The Ohio Review, Harper Studies in Language and Literature, and elsewhere. His first book of stories was published in 1989. His two novels, one collection of three short novels, four collections of short stories, and twenty or so books or chapbooks of poetry have been variously published by Five Fingers, The Crossing Press, Graywolf Press, Standing Stone Books, 2Rivers, BrickHouse Books, Agenda Editions (UK), and Marrowstone. He's been awarded, among other literary honors, two O.Henry's.

Since he entered his eighties, he has declared each new book to be his last with a frequency that embarrasses him. He has not known when or how to stop. It is important to heed one's ghosts. His are telling him here that, since they've known better than he ever has about most things in his life, he should attend to them now, before he's too tired, or fuzzy-headed, to know when to quit himself.

An anecdote:

He has added his middle name, Nissen, for the first time in this book because two of the ghostly voices whispering to him in it are those of his mother, Eva, and her mother, Karen, to whom this book is also dedicated. (See the poem Riddles.)

The original form of the name was Høghnissen, shortened to Nissen by his grandfather when he arrived in the States in his middle fifties, around 1905, and married another Danish immigrant, Karen, then nineteen. His mother was their only child, Danish her first language. As a boy, her father told her, he had read about Lincoln's assassination in a Copenhagen newspaper.

After her mother died in 1946, she had no one left alive to speak it to. It became the silent, interior language of her privacy and solitude.

When she and her husband visited Copenhagen in 1963, he in an "official capacity," they were treated to a great feast during which, a bit tipsy from having been so often toasted as the only woman present, she found herself speaking Danish again, a Danish which a number of the elderly men gathered there told her was lovely to hear, so old-fashioned and formal and, alas, nearly lost to the young.

Even when she was in her late eighties, in a thoughtful, or mournful, mood, she could sometimes be seen staring out a window, whispering to herself in the outdated, vanishing Danish of her early childhood.